BREAKING BAD LOVE HABITS

The Lovers Guide to Creating Passion,
Fire and Everlasting Love in Relationships

ROCHELLE FOXX

©**Copyright 2015 Great Reads Publishing, LLC - All rights reserved.**

This document is geared towards providing exact and reliable information in regards to the topic and issue covered. The publication is sold with the idea that the publisher is not required to render accounting, officially permitted, or otherwise, qualified services. If advice is necessary, legal or professional, a practiced individual in the profession should be ordered.

From a Declaration of Principles which was accepted and approved equally by a Committee of the American Bar Association and a Committee of Publishers and Associations.

In no way is it legal to reproduce, duplicate, or transmit any part of this document in either electronic means or in printed format. Recording of this publication is strictly prohibited and any storage of this document is not allowed unless with written permission from the publisher. All rights reserved.

The information provided herein is stated to be truthful and consistent, in that any liability, in terms of inattention or otherwise, by any usage or abuse of any policies, processes, or directions contained within is the solitary and utter responsibility of the recipient reader. Under no circumstances will any legal responsibility or blame be held against the publisher for any reparation, damages, or monetary loss due to the information herein, either directly or indirectly.

The information herein is offered for informational purposes solely, and is universal as so. The presentation of the information is without contract or any type of guarantee assurance.

The trademarks that are used are without any consent, and the publication of the trademark is without permission or backing by the trademark owner. All trademarks and brands within this book are for clarifying purposes only and are the owned by the owners themselves, not affiliated with this document.

GET YOUR FREE GIFT!

WAIT! – DO YOU LIKE FREE BOOKS?

My **FREE Gift** to You!! As a way to say Thank You for downloading my book, I'd like to offer you more **FREE BOOKS!** Each time we release a NEW book, we offer it first to a small number of people as a test - drive. Because of your commitment here in downloading my book, I'd love for you to be a part of this group. You can join easily here → http://www.rochellefoxx.com

If you're interested in having an *outstandingly passionate relationship* in all areas you **MUST** signup for these **FREE BOOKS!** It's easy to join just by going to my website → http://www.rochellefoxx.com

TABLE OF CONTENTS

Preface 6

CHAPTER 1   Why is Everyone Having More Sex than Me? 10

CHAPTER 2   How Do We as a Couple Define Intimacy and Passion? 14

CHAPTER 3   Common Complaints 16

CHAPTER 4   Why did you fall in love in the first place? 19

CHAPTER 5   Why You Should Stop Thinking – "What can I do?" and Start Thinking "What can we do?" 22

CHAPTER 6   Reevaluate Your Sexual Expectations 25

CHAPTER 7   It's Where You Do It 27

CHAPTER 8   Dare to be Silly 29

CHAPTER 9   Learn Something Together 33

CHAPTER 10   The Importance of Physical Health and Care 36

CHAPTER 11   Positive Body Image 52

CHAPTER 12   Fantasies and Visualization 56

CHAPTER 13   When to Use Pornography 63

CHAPTER 14	Plastic Things That Buzz	66
CHAPTER 15	Mind Your Manners	70
CHAPTER 16	The Art of Flirting	77
CHAPTER 17	Leave Love Notes	80
CHAPTER 18	Take a Break from Each Other	82
CHAPTER 19	Working Around Your "Little Party Crashers"	85
CHAPTER 20	Take a Personality Test	88
CHAPTER 21	Keeping the Mystery Alive	91
CHAPTER 22	Surprise!	94
CHAPTER 23	Take a Technology Diet	96
CHAPTER 24	Benefits of Counseling	100
CHAPTER 25	Organize a "Sexual Retreat"	105
CHAPTER 26	The Mysterious Female Orgasm	109
CHAPTER 27	In Closing	113
References		115
BONUS FOR THE LADIES		119
BONUS FOR THE GUYS		120
Conclusion		121

Preface

Are you currently in a relationship that has lost its' spark? Do you feel apathy where you once held passion and excitement for your partner? Do you believe that your partner feels the same? If the answer is yes one way or the other, you are likely, frustrated, upset, and confused as to how to remedy the situation. Feeling connected to your partner through intimate touch and actions is important for the happiness, health, and longevity of your relationship and every couple deserves this experience. Over time, familiarity, routine, stress, life changes can all affect your level of attraction to one another. Some root causes can be controlled and some cannot; and it is important to recognize the differences so that we can adapt our behaviors accordingly toward positive change. Whether you are married, unmarried, with our without children, these problems can erode our feelings toward our partner and our partner's feelings toward us temporarily. It can be incredibly painful to observe this change in your relationship, and you want to return to the way things were before. As relationships evolve, some flux in levels of attraction and passion are part of the natural rhythms in our lives. However, if it feels there is opportunity to make positive change, and try to get out of an unnaturally long rut, there are several things you can both try to improve the level of passion the two of you share.

It is important to clarify that the intended audience of this book is women who are in a relationship that is deemed safe, free from abuse (mental, physical, emotional, and sexual) and wish to reignite love, passion, and fire in their relationship. Sex and intimacy can never be a resolution to abuse, general lack of interest, or irreconcilable lifestyle differences in a relationship. Sexual activity should never be used as negative reinforcement or manipulation in any way; if so, it will eventually create unpleasant associations for both of you, causing further damage. What sex can do is bring you and your partner together in a universal language of love and passion; when you are physically close, touch one another, show affection, you can bridge many gaps and fortify and validate your feelings for one another.

It's also critical that before putting energy into repairing your sexual relationship with your partner that you still want to be in this relationship. If you are unsure whether you want to continue with the relationship, you should first evaluate whether or not you wish to remain with your partner. We all have personal limits and boundaries of which we should not push or allow others to push. It is also important to take a step back and determine if there are deeper issues which need to be addressed of which decreased desire and passion are symptoms. If you feel you do not want to remain, the advice provided is not intended to rescue a relationship which is at its end. If there is no desire to stay, from either or both partners, working on your sexual relationship is a moot point.

A healthy relationship is more than physical intimacy and sex, as you know, and the root of passion and love is a culmination of all the other elements being in place. This book also assumes that passion and sexual intimacy were present at the onset of the relationship and that a sexual relationship has already been established at some point. The advice and ideas provided are most helpful for couples that have been together for some time as opposed to newer relationships. Recognizing the symptoms of waning attraction is the first step, understanding your partner's nature and behavior, motivations and preferences comes with time. You'll want to be confident that any method you employ to reignite passion will address one of the main causes; and that takes intimate knowledge and familiarity with your partner, and your own role in the relationship. It is my sincere hope that this book can bring joy and closeness back to you and your partner if you are experiencing difficulty. If you are simply curious and want to add a little more "oomph" to your sex life, you will also benefit. Passion is what keeps us intrigued, interested, motivated and coming back for more. Above all else, remember that sex is healthy and sex should be fun!

CHAPTER 1

WHY IS EVERYONE HAVING MORE SEX THAN ME?

When you think about the level of passion and the amount of sex you are having in your relationship, you must first determine whether you are comparing it to your own history as a couple or to your perception of other couples. You are likely wondering "what is a healthy amount of sex?," "are other couples having more sex than us?" and "when should I be worried?" There's a difference between a short "sex famine" and a recurring theme. Not having sex doesn't mean you aren't deeply in love but multiple studies demonstrate that lack of sex is closely related to dissatisfaction or thoughts of leaving the relationship. Frequency of sex reduces as our age increases; this is a natural pattern. According to the Kinsey Institute, "a study of married couples found age and marital satisfaction to be the two variables most associated with amount of sex. […]Across all ages couples who reported higher levels of marital satisfaction also reported higher frequencies of sex. (Call, 1995)."

According to the Kinsey Institute, a renowned and reputable institute specializing in human sexual behavior research, women report a decreasing frequency of sexual intercourse as they age and are in partnered and married relationships. Using this information as appoint of reference, you can gain some insight as to what is average for couples in your age group.

Percentage of Women Reporting Frequency of Vaginal Sex, N=2393							
Age Group	18-24	25-29	30-39	40-49	50-59	60-69	70+
Single							
Not in past year	50.8	43.0	72.3	71.1	85.4	84.5	100.0
A few times per year to monthly	16.4	21.5	10.7	16.9	5.4	6.5	0.0
A few times per month to weekly	19.7	24.1	12.5	9.9	7.0	6.5	0.0
2-3 times per week	8.2	1.3	4.5	2.1	2.2	2.6	0.0
4 or more times per week	4.9	10.1	0.0	0.0	0.0	0.0	0.0
Partnered							
Not in past year	12.9	10.6	14.8	20.6	21.1	14.8	30.8
A few times per year to monthly	16.1	11.7	13.6	13.7	18.3	11.1	15.4

A few times per month to weekly	31.2	36.2	43.2	24.5	36.6	48.1	23.1
2-3 times per week	32.3	28.7	18.2	31.4	18.3	18.5	7.7
4 or more times per week	7.5	12.8	10.2	9.8	5.6	7.4	23.1
Married							
Not in past year	11.8	3.5	6.5	8.1	22.0	37.9	53.5
A few times per year to monthly	14.7	11.6	16.3	21.7	23.7	20.0	25.4
A few times per month to weekly	14.7	47.7	50.2	46.6	36.2	35.9	18.3
2-3 times per week	35.3	35.2	21.9	20.8	16.9	6.2	1.4
4 or more times per week	23.5	2.0	5.1	2.7	1.1	0.0	1.4

NSSHB, 2010, excerpted from "Sexual Behaviors, Relationships, and Perceived Health Among Adult Men in the United States: Results from a National Probability Sample", Table 6.

If you feel your emotional connection is strong, and you have noticed a drastic decrease in the amount of sex you expect and need in order to feel satisfied with your partner, you should consider trying to make some changes in your behavior.

A decrease in regular sexual activity can be symptomatic of numerous things, some you can control and some you cannot. Before you try any behavioral modifications, take time to evaluate the factors that could be influencing the libido of you and / or your partner:

- Health: physical, mental, emotional health

- Medications: many medications are known to reduce libido and energy levels. Check the medications you and your partner are taking for such side effects.

- Family Demands: if you have young children or family members for whom you are caring, this can greatly disrupt your sexual schedule and desire.

- Work & Stress: the pressures and stress of work and the combination of having to financially support yourself and others can very easily annihilate desire.

- Lack of Trust: Are you or your partner keeping things from one another? Do you feel there are unspoken or unknown facets of your lives that cause suspicion and or erode trust?

All of the above are unique circumstances but are those in which typically cannot cause further deterioration by employing the enclosed suggestions and ideas in this book.

CHAPTER 2

HOW DO WE AS A COUPLE DEFINE INTIMACY AND PASSION?

Love notes, hugs, holding hands, spontaneous sex, subtle gestures... It is important to understand how you and your partner communicate love and intimacy. Your perceptions and needs may be different and you could be delivering your messages in a way in which the other partner is not programmed to receive them. Passion is fueled by mutually understood expressions of love. Do you and your partner speak the same love language? If not, are you aware of the differences and do you make time to appreciate the gestures used by your partner to express love? There are some very helpful books on these differences that can help set you up for better understanding the different expressions of love. The Five Love Languages: How to Express Heartfelt

Commitment to Your Mate by Gary Chapman, is a well respected resource for helping people speak and understand emotional love when it is expressed through one of five languages: words of affirmation, quality time, receiving gifts, acts of service, or physical touch. One of the key tenants of the book is that when expressing love toward your partner, you should do your best not to default to the love language that *you* prefer, but instead use the language that your partner is able to receive and understand. Using the idea of love language as a starting point, some of these tips and ideas may or may not work based on how your partner prefers to receive love. However, since this book focuses on reigniting physical passion, there will be more content around the physical love language and quality time.

CHAPTER 3

COMMON COMPLAINTS

- "Lovemaking is like a chore for us."
- "It lacks spontaneity."
- "My partner lacks interest in me sexually."
- "I lack sexual interest in my partner."
- "I am no longer physically attracted to my partner."

If any of these expressions describes how you are feeling in your relationship, you can benefit by employing some or all of the suggestions I'd like to share with you.

In some scenarios, a partner can believe that by giving the other what they need may result in it being taken for granted and being simply taken, this "emotionally bankrupting" the giver. That the receiver will take without reciprocation. One bad experience can put a person in the habit of counting the "cost" or potential risk of everything they give to their partner emotionally or physically. In other scenarios, some couples know exactly what the other needs sexually or emotionally and begin to withhold it to manipulate other aspects of the relationship. In any type of withholding, both of you starve. I want to make this point as the next step in understanding each other's love language is to use it in a healthy manner and to communicate love rather than to deplete it. This phrase resonates particularly loudly within this context; "'Change so I can change,' argues the fool."

Those of you who have been close to someone long enough to know both the awe inspiring and the apathetic morass of long-term partner relationships, you can attest to the fact that at some point, you will question the longevity of the passion and fervor of the relationship. "Will it satisfy me beyond today, beyond the next few months, for the next year, for a lifetime?" "Does this relationship excite me emotionally, sexually, and intellectually enough to sustain me and does it exceed my limits as a partner?"

You can feel love, gratefulness, respect, appreciation, and safety with your partner yet not feel sexually excited or inspired. These feelings are common among the modern woman who juggles a multitude of externally and internally imposed limitations. A stipulation is that you want to continue and that you see a future in the relationship before you put your precious energy into rescuing a waning passion between you and your partner. Sometimes the answer to matters of the heart is as simple as careful observation of your environment, your reactions, and your past experiences. If you feel the relationship is healthy for you and your partner, you can consider one or more of the methods provided to get you back into that blissful closeness you knew in the beginning.

CHAPTER 4

WHY DID YOU FALL IN LOVE IN THE FIRST PLACE?

Take some time to think about and / or write down the reasons why you invited this person into your life. Why were they worth your time and energy; how did he/she inspire you? Did they make you laugh, lean in and listen more than anyone else in the room? Could they finish your sentences... did you feel like you were old souls together? Do you share such similar interests you felt you had a companion in your favorite activities? Or was it simply raw animal attraction? Perhaps you grew to know and love one another slowly, through mutual friends.

Either scenario, it is an important first step to evaluate who you were when you met and who you are now. Consider how your paths have diverged or converged over time. It may help to write down these comparisons. Try to understand why you feel that affection has waned. Over time, it is easy to take for granted why you both made the decision to share your deepest self with another person. As we grow and mature, it isn't uncommon to grow in different directions. A good friend of mine elegantly explained her and her girlfriend's mutual decision to separate simply by stating, "We grew in completely different ways. Seven years later, we realized we were vastly different and were no longer compatible." Take note whether the characteristics you first loved in your partner are still present, then make a point to notably appreciate this in your partner. Remind them why you fell in love and reassure them that you still love these aspects of their personality. But what if you and your partner have experienced a great deal of change over time? If they have evolved and you find this growth to be positive, be sure to share your observation and acknowledge that the change is something you love and / or are learning to love. It sounds quite simple and straightforward, but can be quite difficult to step back and make this comparison. Revisit your history together, but don't let it history limit your development as a couple – focus only on the positive in this exercise. You can do nothing but good in sharing positive sentiment with your partner. This can help remind you why you couldn't keep your minds (and hands) off one another when you met... or come up with new reasons to keep going strong.

CHAPTER 5

WHY YOU SHOULD STOP THINKING – "WHAT CAN I DO?" AND START THINKING "WHAT CAN WE DO?"

A common misconception in modern relationships is the "superwoman complex" in which we women feel it is our responsibility to maintain the passion in our relationships. We flog ourselves emotionally for being too tired, too anxious, or inhabiting a body we don't perceive as "sexy enough" to put us in an ideal setting for intimacy. We blame ourselves for not being in a sexual mood at the "right time," and we beat ourselves up over how we think others believe we should act or perceive us as sexual beings. The biggest misconception is that there is an ideal setting, time, level of fitness to be a sexual being; that is a limitation which inevitably prevents the spontaneity and excitement that relationships require to fuel ongoing passion. Perhaps you impose these limitations on yourself and are focusing on a fictitious and ideal environment for sex.

Try your best to put those thoughts aside for a time and try to coach yourself into an alternate mindset. A more healthy approach is to determine when you and your partner are at your most and least receptive to being physically close. You can do this by simply reflecting on or observing when your partner is receptive to sexual intimacy and when they are not. Next, turn this observation on yourself and your patterns. Do you prefer not to be physical after meals? Do you feel self conscious in the morning or in bright light? Is your partner more receptive after socializing with others or after a few hours relaxing alone with you? Perhaps there is some unspoken resentment held that is preventing feelings of trust and intimacy? Do you love to be close during the work week or during your time off? In comparison, do you find that you and your partner have complimentary or opposing patterns of sexual receptiveness? Understand your patterns, physically and emotionally, then share this with your partner and encourage them to do the same. Spend some time exploring how the two of you can better understand the root cause of the blockage preventing sexual intimacy. If you have opposing patterns, you can try some gentle compromise. What are the non-negotiable limits for both of you? If there are any, be sensitive and don't push the hard limits. Focus on the aspects on which you and your partner can meet in the middle and broaden your receptive sweet spot. By being aware of these differences, you will likely become more open minded to timing and setting best suited for you as a couple. You may even discover that timing, place, or scenario out of the norm will be exactly what you both need.

CHAPTER 6

REEVALUATE YOUR SEXUAL EXPECTATIONS

A healthy and realistic relationship waxes and wanes though periods of passion and fulfillment into periods or platonic partnership and back again. If the two of you were forever ensconced in the "honeymoon phase" neither of you would get anything done! You wouldn't realistically be able to participate in a larger and fuller life or accomplish many of the goals you set for yourself outside of your partnership. Take time to remind yourself of this. You and your partner can't always have turbo-charged sex drives because we have a finite amount of time and energy to spend on the things we love, including your partner. Would you love your partner if they couldn't be the best version of their self? In turn, would you resent your partner if they prevented you from your own goals to grow and accomplish? Contemplate whether you and your partner have achieved a healthy balance in spending time on your independent lives as well as your sexual lives. What did this look like? Now come to the present and conduct the same evaluation. If you find that time you and your partner have previously spent on sexual and intimate activity is now focused elsewhere, try to define where it is being spent. Is it being spent productively and positively for the relationship or an individual's needs / goals? If so, allow the space and time to revel in the personal progress you both are making. Bring this observation to your partner and make a point to positively acknowledge the focus. Then you can suggest that the two of you make efforts to devote more time to one another. Pour a whiskey or go for a long walk and make a point to share why you love each other outside of the relationship. Why do you feel proud to stand beside him / her? Don't compare your sexual selves to the honeymoon phase; try to take intimacy outside of the bedroom and reintroduce it through rediscovery and appreciation for the person who exists beyond the sexual. It takes time and effort, but you will find the reflected adoration will spark a desire to be closer, physically.

CHAPTER 7

IT'S WHERE YOU DO IT

Psychologically, we revert to behavioral schemas when triggered by stimuli. Your environment provides key stimuli in feelings of sexual preparation and arousal. There are benefits to a familiar setting, like feelings of comfort, safety, and privacy. However, the detriment is that you can come to an impasse where contact outside of these schemas fails to occur to you or your partner and hence, prevent the renewal of excitement and novelty common to a young relationship. Do you find that you and you partner only kiss or touch in specific environments or places like the bedroom, living room, or in your vehicles alone? Not all of us are willing to tease the line of exhibition but there are acceptable limits that we can toy with that will upset the tired scenarios in which we anticipate or are prepared for arousal. Have you shared a passionate kiss in an empty elevator? Would you rub each other's feet under the tablecloth at a restaurant? Do you feel comfortable suggestively nuzzling the ear of your lover on the subway? Be creative in where you show passion, try to surprise your partner, and encourage them to do the same to you while respecting one another's limits. It will shock you out of old patterns and make you both more receptive to spontaneous gestures of love.

CHAPTER 8

DARE TO BE SILLY

Laughter is the best medicine… and it's a strong aphrodisiac. Laughter relaxes us, makes us forget our problems for a time, can repair emotional damage, and just feels good. As a couple, you have collected countless shared experiences, and undoubtedly some are downright hilarious. Inside jokes are one of the most beautiful and binding facets of close relationships. They can be innocent, raunchy, absurd, or deeply meaningful. No one really gets it but the two of you and no one ever will. This is one of your strengths as a couple and you should both use this to your advantage as it instills closeness and intimacy. The same applies to sex… if you or your partner think it has to be bosom heaving, serious love-making all the time, you're doing it wrong. That mindset prevents you both from your deepest pleasure and sets a false pretence for intimacy because neither of you will feel genuine in the moment.

Studies on sexual selection theory and human behavior sexual have indicated that humor ability is one of the top three traits in mate selection. A good sense of humor is a social and interpersonal trait involving interpretation of cues, timing, awareness of audience, and intelligence. Studies have strongly correlated humor ability with intelligence, which is a highly desirable trait in mate selection. An interesting difference in sexual preference is that women respond more positively to others (of both sexes) who produce humor, whereas men respond most positively to those who are receptive to their own humor (Bressler & Martin, 2006.) This doesn't mean that as a woman, you should laugh at all your man's jokes (that's way too close to some outdated and sexist relationship advice) but understand that if your male partner is using a lot of humor, it can often mean he is trying to impress you and bond with you either consciously or subconsciously. Recognize this and try to reciprocate, encourage it, and know that when you and your partner laugh together, it can solidify your bond.

I haven't found a single couple that says they want to laugh less. Unfortunately much of our humor these days comes in the form of internet memes, TV laugh track scripted sitcoms, and satirical blogs. To derive the best and most genuine bonding experience from humor is to further develop your home grown version. Most of what we find humorous isn't the "laugh out loud" variety, but what can be derived from natural conversation and comments. Laughter, although difficult to study and dissect, it is key in social relationships and is also sexual ones because it strengthens the relationship as it validates shared opinions.

It seems like common sense that fun and gentle humor should be welcome bedfellows. The social benefits are obvious, but what about the physical ones? There are many parallels between the physical benefits of both laughter and sex. Both boost mood-altering chemicals that combat stress and depression and lower stress related hormones like cortisone and adrenaline. Particularly in women, skin sensitivity increases during laughter and sexual activity; the relief and relaxation women feel after both is physiologically similar.

That said, never poke fun at your partner, but use your private "language" as a couple to make each other laugh, and feel at home in your bodies. Nowhere are our egos more delicate than in the bedroom so avoid sarcasm, jokes about one another, your partner's body, and anything that could be perceived as mean-spirited. Humor during sex is best received in established couples, where as in newer relationships nervous laughter can be misconstrued.

History and familiarity provide a wide variety of topics which are tested and true; you and your partner know what makes the other giggle, and what can fall flat. So next time you are together and things feel too stern or pressured try to take a break from intercourse by touching and caressing while talking and joking together. It will relax you both and bring the best parts of your relationship into the part that needs a little care and bring you closer as a couple.

CHAPTER 9

LEARN SOMETHING TOGETHER

Boring people have boring sex. Have one or both of you stopped trying to experience or learn new things (outside of the bedroom?) If you're not actively trying to learn anything new or seeking new experiences, you are likely not growing as a person either. Sharing a learning experience with your partner can help reconnect you as a couple and reintroduce the novelty of getting to know and grow with one another that you felt early on. When you stop growing and evolving as a person, one or both of you can become bored and disenchanted with the relationship. The excitement and novelty can translate to the bedroom.

One of the best activities for couples to begin with is cooking. Because cooking and meal preparation are necessary activities, you're doing something together that you're going to do something together and save precious time working as a team, it is easy to introduce as a learning experience. By cooking together you exercise planning, teamwork, and communication which is important to practice and refine in your relationship in general. Cooking is generally a nonthreatening activity and a great way to blend your tastes and styles and show off your skills to impress your partner. It can be artistic, creative, have varying complexity levels, and there are endless possibilities for continued learning. Plus, you get to enjoy the product of your hard work together as a couple!

Depending on your levels of physical fitness and body security, taking up a physical challenge together can be an incredible way to refresh your appreciation for one another's bodies. At first it can make you insecure to be sweating and exerting yourself in front of your partner... if either of you are worried about this, perhaps that fear is also holding you or your partner back in another area involving lots of physical exertion; sex. This makes it all the more compelling reason to put on your work out gear and get moving. I'm a huge fan of yoga, kayaking, and hiking. My current boyfriend is an avid mountain biker and snowboarder. I know one of his favorite ways to spend time with me is outside... which can be intimidating because we are on very different planes, physically. He won't be caught dead at the yoga studio, and there is no way I am risking a broken leg on the slopes; those are our limits. But we're happiest when hiking or walking in the woods together. I stretched my limits when I agreed to start snow shoeing with him this winter and much to my surprise, I really enjoy it. Thankfully he's patient with my learning curve, and he loves teaching me. Conversely, he's not so skilled at kayaking, so the tables are turned when we hit the lake or river, but he's so excited to be sharing an experience with me doing something outside, that he's ok not being number one.

CHAPTER 10

THE IMPORTANCE OF PHYSICAL HEALTH AND CARE

This topic is a great bridge between learning something together and improving your physical health. Couples who work out together can save time and avoid the conflicting decision between working out and spending time with their partner. But let's get to the good stuff... Couples who work out together have better sex lives. Not only are they building body confidence, but it increases testosterone levels in both sexes which directly increases sex drive. Your energy level will increase, and the "feel good" chemicals, endorphins, are released through increased and strenuous physical activity. Not only does exercise boost energy levels but it helps alleviate depression and fatigue, two common culprits in the erosion of sex drive. If you and your partner are at different levels of fitness, try an activity in which you can both be together, but work at your individual level. Great examples of these are spinning classes, mid-level yoga (where there are many modifications offered) and using cardio equipment together. For most of us, one of the things we have control over is our physical fitness relative to our age, it is also one of the biggest things to let slip when we get settled in to a relationship because we get comfortable with our partner and comfortable with seeing each others' bodies. Working out together not only helps you both look and feel your best but you are able to encourage each other and share an experience with your partner.

Physical health is of course more than just having a strong body, it involves accepting and acting on a lifestyle of choices that are best for our bodies and minds. Enjoying food and drink is one of the most common social activities for couples. It's also how many of us relax after a long day. However, as we settle in to the relationship it is common to realize that both of your eating habits have changed for the worse; more rich fatty foods, alcohol consumption increases, sodium intake, and sugar intake all increase because we enjoy these foods together. It is particularly difficult for live-in partners to have separate eating habits as when one eats or drinks, the other commonly joins in. Studies show that couples will consume up to 33% more calories in the presence of their partner than they would than merely eating alone. Couples are also 37% more likely to become obese if their partner becomes obese. If you and your partner are struggling with attraction primarily due to your physical attraction and weight, a great place to start is at the dinner table. Not only does making a promise to one another to eat healthier give you something to work towards and learn, but you each hold one another accountable for and cheer each other on in attaining a healthier physique and lifestyle.

Try to kick or reduce bad habits such as excessive drinking and smoking. Alcohol may temporarily lift our inhibitions, but it kills sexual performance as it is a depressant. Alcohol slows down a man's ability to achieve and hold an erection and slows down or even prevents the vagina from lubricating. High blood alcohol levels have been linked to delayed orgasm and decreased sexual sensitivity. So if you and your partner are already having a difficult time with sexual pleasure, more than a couple drinks can ruin your plans for an exciting and intimate encounter. If performance is a difficulty in your relationship and either of you is a smoker, there is a strong case to quit. Sexual arousal and performance relies on vasodilatation and unobstructed blood flow to the pelvic area and genitals. Nicotine constricts blood vessels as well as increases the formation of atherosclerotic plaque on the vessel walls, further preventing proper blood flow. Additionally, reports indicate that smoking damages the smooth muscle tissue inside the sexual organs required for erectile functioning.

Recreational and prescription drugs can do a lot of damage not only to your body and brain, but to your sexual health. Be aware that antihistamines, sedatives, and opiates depress and can "numb" sexual sensitivity by causing drowsiness, reducing lubrication, and decreasing energy levels. Marijuana, although relaxing for many can not only cause the infamous "dry mouth" but can dry you down south as well. Stay away from pot if you are trying to put the charge back in your love life. Talk to your doctor about the side effects of the prescriptions you or your partner are taking and determine if these are the culprits behind a stagnant sex life. Literature and research around the sexual side effects of prescription and recreational drugs is plentiful; a good first step is to list all the medications and drugs you and your partner are taking to determine what and how it can affect the two of you. As this isn't a medical text, I would encourage you to seek out peer reviewed and researched information sources on these medications. There are advances and options available that may be options and substitutes for any medications that are putting you and your partner at risk for depressed libido.

Proper nutrition is critical for sexual health. We aren't talking fabled aphrodisiac foods but honest to goodness nutritional evidence for sexual health. It's difficult to disagree that healthy hormone levels, a healthy nervous system and circulatory health in the pelvic area are essential to experiencing a healthy sex drive.

Did you know that poor posture can reduce sex drive? It sounds unrelated at first; but consider what a slouch does to our mood, confidence, and comfort. We breathe shallowly when we are bent over a computer, desk, or our smartphones. This not only reduces oxygen levels in our bloodstreams but increases feelings of stress and cortisol, but also reduces energy and the release of testosterone in our bloodstream. (Low testosterone levels in both men and women are correlated to reduced sex drive. Cortisol is a hormone released by increased stress levels and is worth your time in researching if you feel stress is a big factor in your sexual difficulty.) Improving your posture is oddly linked to our libidos, but it makes perfect sense that with improved posture comes a more positive self image. Both you and your partner look and feel your best when standing and sitting comfortably but properly.

When was the last time (if every) you had comprehensive blood analysis performed? As a follow up to many of the above topics, blood analysis can shed light on potential health and nutritional issues that affect our sexual health. For example, even slightly decreased THS levels can bring about fatigue, decreased, libido, and depression. Hypothyroidism shows down the metabolism and causes the adrenal glands to produce less of the hormones that are precursors to sex hormones testosterone and estrogen. Zinc, Iron, and vitamin E deficiencies have also been linked to decreased libido in both sexes. Your doctor can order a blood panel that can reveal nutritional and other hormonal factors influencing your libido.

Are you and your partner getting enough sleep? Less sleep may mean less sex. Lack of sleep can wreak havoc on your work, your social life, and your sex life. The tension and anxiety that accompany sleeplessness are legitimate libido killers. As a fellow sufferer of insomnia, I am very passionate about this topic. Lack of sleep makes us grumpy, irritable, and when we are deprived of it, we want nothing to do with sex. Interestingly, sleep apnea, the inability to breathe properly while sleeping, is shown to reduce testosterone levels in men, particularly during the restorative hours of the night. Whether or not this is an effect of poor sleep quality or the stress on the body due to breathing interference, it is a factor to consider. Over time, sleep deprivation can contribute to depression which, as we have covered in several areas, reduces sexual desire and ability to experience orgasm. Sleep and sleeping habits can truly come between couples; one partner sleeps like a rock while the other tosses and turns. This can cause confusion and resentment among partners when one cannot understand why the other has so much difficulty and the one with insomnia is frustrated with the others inability to empathize. Sleep and lack thereof has such a significant impact on our lives; many people with insomnia have developed elaborate routines and sensitivities to sleeping environments and preparation. In my own relationships, I have had difficulty explaining my own chronic insomnia and sensitivities to my partners. I will give up just about anything for uninterrupted sleep, sex and food included, and this has caused me and my partners a great deal of strain particularly when it comes to sex drive. I have the luxury of having another sleeping area in my home to which I can escape if I need to be away from my partner and I understand not everyone has this. However, designating a place where you or your partner can go to when you can't share a bed truly helps the situation. I made it very clear that sleep was part of my health and hygiene, and that my need for sleep was not personal and it deeply upset me if I couldn't get a proper amount or if I felt I was facing a sleepless night. I was very clear in communicating that this was one of my must haves and ground rules for my happiness and well-being, and that it prevented me from having interest in anything else if I couldn't sleep, particularly sex. For some partners it takes a bit of acclimation when I chose to sleep elsewhere, and at first they took it personally. I made a point to cuddle and spend time with them for a while in bed, read and talk quietly, until my partner was drowsy enough to fall asleep. This was a good compromise for us on those nights when I couldn't bear to share a bed for fear of insomnia. They felt loved and the cozy intimacy of bedtime as a couple, but neither of us suffered for my lack of sleep. If you or your partner suffer from sleep problems talk about how to set up an environment where sleep is possible both together and separately. Discuss your sleeping preferences and what you need to feel relaxed. Invest in earplugs and a good mattress, quality bedding, and tranquil settings. Not only will you sleep better, but the bed and the bedroom won't become triggers for anxiety, triggers that have you conditioned to feel negative emotions towards the bedroom which is for sleep, relaxation, and sex.

Outside of the things we can do to maintain and improve our health and sexual experiences, what about our perceptions of what makes our partner attractive, and what attracts our partner to us? While the adage states that beauty is in the eye of the beholder, and that it is more than skin deep, there is no fault in being honest about what physical triggers are important to our ability to be attracted to someone. We all have physical characteristics which we must accept as permanent and some over which we have control. Take some time to recall what aspects of your lover's physical self turned you on when you first met and next determine what you find attractive today. Are these aspects different? Are the factors influencing these changes under the control of your partner or not? It is unfair to expect our partners not to show signs of aging, or experience physical changes after childbirth, life events, health episodes or conditions. We have to be willing to accept these changes in our partners just as we want them to be accepted in ourselves. Granted, there are factors over which we can control and those we cannot. For those that we can control, or believe our partner can control, a little effort goes a long way. Granted, no one wants the answer to "Honey, do you think I look good in this?" to be "Umm… actually…no." Delivery is so important when admitting that you may not be as attracted to your partner as you were before. No one wants to hear this news however, sometimes it is necessary. If it was something that could be changed, wouldn't you be grateful for that honesty rather than letting it continue to erode your sexual feelings? There are some steps to initiating this conversation.

Spend time figuring out where you're coming from. What physical aspects in partners or potential partners were you attracted to before you met your current partner? Conversely, what physical aspects were deal-breakers for you? Do you feel that you were willing to compromise these preferences to accommodate your partner?

Identify something that can be constructively improved. Weight gain, poor hygiene, and unflattering clothing / style, are the most common complaints. An example of constructively approaching weight gain is to focus on health, not weight; talk about the benefits outside of merely looking more attractive. Perhaps there is a change in your lifestyles or available time that makes it more difficult to stay at a healthy and attractive size. Be cautious about where you bring this up, avoid before or during sex… as it can really make your partner upset and kill any chance of a constructive conversation about improving your love lives and mutual attraction. If your partner can open up to you about this, it's your collective responsibility to try to come up with solutions to promote a healthier lifestyle.

Hygiene is another one that can slip when you get comfortable with one another. Funky smells, unclean clothing, excess hair, bad breath… these can kill an intimate moment in a heartbeat. I had a boyfriend who I had to confront about his bedding and laundry. It got really awkward when I refused to stay over and he couldn't figure out why even after all the hints that his sheets and laundry smelled unpleasant. Finally, I explained to him that I can't sleep unless the bed is clean and that it was also upsetting to me to be naked anywhere near that bed… no self-respecting woman wants her delicate lady parts on dirty linens. I asked him to please wash the sheets for me and I promised I'd spend time with him between them. It worked.

Positive reinforcement and encouragement are the best ways to promote healthier and better grooming in your partner. I love my boyfriend very much, but he is an uncommonly hairy man, which is not my personal preference, but that's what I've got to work with and I've come to love it as just another quirky part of him. When we first started dating, he had been single for some time and had some wild body hair that was definitely in need of management. Some of it is just the way he's built, but there was a big opportunity for grooming; I wanted to get him to maintain a reasonable grooming regimen without asking him to go to great efforts (extreme shaving and electrolysis would be hurtful suggestions.) What I did was spend a lot of time adoring the parts of him that were well groomed, and when we were getting ready one evening, I told him I really wanted to be able to feel more of his skin, that it would help me feel closer to him, and asked if he could please try trimming. This was incentive enough, and when I delivered on my appreciation of his newly reachable chest (etc.) he has kept it up with minimal effort as part of his regular routine. However, this also came back to me one winter when I was getting very lazy about my own body hair. He chose a much less subtle approach in communicating his preference to me by purchasing a very fancy razor to replace my disposable ones. His line was that he knew I cut myself often shaving and wouldn't this be a nice change? I got the hint and now keep up my end of the deal.

If you live together or spend a lot of time in each other's homes, you can find you rarely see each other outside of your pajamas, or old sweatpants and holey t-shirts. I am all for being comfortable, and all couples should be ok with loosening up and being natural. I am one of the guiltiest people of this whereas my boyfriend is most relaxed in a blazer, jeans, and beautifully polished shoes even when around the home. I am aware that I can look like I just crawled out of bed at 4pm when I work from home, and half the time I have no qualms about it. But I know it not only pleases him to see me more polished, but a little makeup, a more polished version of comfort (like jeans and a cozy sweater) make me feel more desirable as well. I always make a point to dress appropriately when I go out in public so why not give him my best self on occasion? The effort to be attractive for my partner typically doesn't go unnoticed. If you want your partner to improve their personal style, start dressing with the same level of effort you did when you started dating, by bumping it up a notch yourself, you can subtly encourage your partner to make the same improvements. Be sensitive about trying to influence your partner's style too much; the way we dress can be a large part of our self expression and identity and by overly criticizing it, we can send the message that the other person's expression of identity is undesirable and unattractive. This is one of those tricky areas where it can't happen overnight and is largely influenced by positive reinforcement by you and others. It can be scary to disrupt our dressing habits, we get used to the look and feel of certain clothing and are hesitant to change. We all know someone like this, someone who is be stuck in the fashions and styles of a long past decade and refuses or doesn't see the need to change. Over time it can be embarrassing to be seen with this person, or makes us uncomfortable because it draws negative attention from others. Shopping together, as leisurely as possible, and with minimal pressure can be one way to slowly get your partner to update their fashion repertoire. Use encouragement, and be sure to genuinely tell them how attractive they are to you in more appropriate clothing and styles. Never force a partner to wear something new, or set ultimatums about self-expression through clothing and style. This will only undermine your efforts to help them look and feel better. When and if they get the courage to branch out, be sure that they can start out in baby steps; not all at once and don't ask them to shake it up too much at an important or high pressure event where they will become even more self-conscious. Your efforts can seriously backfire if they try something new and then associate it with an unpleasant social experience or negative attention. Be gentle and encouraging with your partner at all times as changing a habit is a slow process.

If you get the impression that you yourself may need a bit of a makeover, take a long hard look in the mirror, have you let yourself go? Also, enlist the opinions of good friends to determine if your impressions are valid. There are many ways to make yourself more stylish and freshen up your look without compromising the things which make you look and feel yourself. Makeover shows are popular for a reason: it's an amazing and more often than not, positive, transformation. Men particularly respond to improved attractiveness in their partners, they love to see you do something new with your hair, makeup, clothing because they not only enjoy novelty, but when you exude confidence you are also more sexually appealing. Maybe a small makeover is just what you need to pique his interest in you sexually again. You won't be comfortable if you change everything all at once, so I recommend tweaking the things which you feel can be reversible if you don't feel ok with the change. A few updates to your wardrobe by pulling out unflattering clothing from your closet and bringing a good friend along to help you pick out new flattering styles is an easy one. Making small changes to your makeup style and beauty regimen are also very easy to incorporate. You can also speak to your hairdresser about new ways to style your existing cut in order to flatter your face shape and perhaps discuss other complimentary cuts for your contours. In one of my former relationships I realized that my partner thought I had beautiful hair and wanted me to wear it down more often as he preferred it that way. I had been having it pulled back because for me, it is more comfortable, but I made sure to occasionally make some effort to wear it the way he liked it on dates or times when we were together. He liked being able to touch it and enjoyed how I looked. Granted, it was back in a ponytail shortly, but even that small bit of acknowledgement of what he found sexy was positive for us. Just remember, as uncomfortable as it is for you to change up your style habits, it is equally as difficult for your partner. No one should have to change everything and compromise their identity, but a few tweaks here and there can really help you both feel sexier and more attracted to one another.

CHAPTER 11

POSITIVE BODY IMAGE

This may sound contradictory after the former topics of physical health, and the two are not mutually exclusive, yet I know many women with healthy bodies that do not love their body or image. I also know many men who have the same self perception. Think about the number of women you know who have a healthy view of their beautifully imperfect body and then compare it to the number you know who are openly critical of every flaw. Even if she is attractive by most standards, and her partner has a positive view of her, a woman's libido takes a plunge if she doesn't believe she is "sexy looking" enough. Now more than ever, our exposure to media and its continuous and pervasive presence makes it impossible to escape the influence of idealized and nearly impossible beauty. We see images of people who make a career out of being coiffed and styled, fit, trained, and groomed for viewers pleasure. These people are not subject to the time pressures and physical rigor of normal life. They are also selected for exceptional physical traits and / or transformational ability... like a canvas. They are career beauties. There will always be someone we feel is more attractive than us. We need to accept that and accept that wanting it or our partner wanting it is an unrealistic expectation. As above, this doesn't mean we can forgo health and wellness and grooming hoping someone will love us regardless... that is equally unrealistic. Self-criticism is harmful more than it is helpful and many of us use it as a reason for waning sexual desire. How do we change the negative criticism and reclaim our right to feel sexual and at home in our bodies? Anxiety kills pleasure. First and foremost, you need to work on the aspects of your body image that cause you the most anxiety. Oftentimes we are most anxious over what we believe is excess fat in areas where our partner loves to touch. We won't let them see or touch these otherwise erogenous areas for fear of judgment and comparison. Belly, butt, thighs, inner arms... all sensitive areas we fixate on as imperfect or too fat. We ban our own pleasure and we also ban our partners pleasure when we no longer permit sexual touch in these areas. It's important to focus on the way things feel first before you can be more comfortable being seen. Sex in the dark, and asking for lights off sex is completely acceptable. If you are afraid of asking for the true reason, you can phrase it as what it truly is, "I would like to focus on feeling alone tonight. I'd like to just feel you and have you feel me." You may find that some of the pressure dissolves. Conversely, you may be dealing with negative body image held by your partner. You can create an environment of acceptance similarly to asking for one yourself. You can ensure your partner knows that you are excited by their body and remind them that you can understand why they feel the way they do but even if what they see as imperfections or flaws are inhibiting them, it's not apparent to or inhibiting you. Invest in lighting with dimmers. Invest in good candles; both things you can use to control how visually exposed you feel as you become more assured your partner loves your body. The goal is to begin to see your body as your own sexual and sensual instrument. When I am experiencing self doubt and less than positive body image I remind myself how wonderful it is to live in a healthy, mobile, body that does all the things I like to do, and takes me places I want to go. Even when I am physically not my healthiest, I set realistic expectations base on medical advice, surround myself with body positive media, and body positive people. A trend in my advice is media dieting. I honestly believe that our exposure to so many comparative others (people, scenarios, lifestyles, class, options, products, and ideas) can shake our fundamental cores and confidence. It's not that we are weak and susceptible, but that the influx is so strong and in such quantity that is takes a near super-human effort not to experience its effects. Picture a tree in a strong wind. It can bend, and it wavers and is built to take a buffeting on occasion, but if those winds were too strong or lasted too long, the tree would eventually break. We need to give ourselves a break from that pressure… or we need to reinforce our confidence. The latter takes time and experience.

CHAPTER 12

FANTASIES AND VISUALIZATION

Creating and utilizing sexual fantasies involving your partner takes practice, imagination, and time. If you and your partner lack sexual interest, you're going to struggle with this one more than others. At first it will feel silly and painful; you'll feel it is being forced. But making a discipline out of sexual daydreaming can give you the charge you need to feel sexually excited by your partner. We women are primarily wired to enjoy the buildup of sexual excitement during the time leading up to a sexual act. Fantasizing can slowly and steadily put you in a receptive mood to be close to your partner. This is particularly helpful (but not limited to) heterosexual relationships in which a male partner can be sexually ready quite rapidly. Remember, we are focusing on your passion as well as your partner's! Fantasies can be anything you wish them to be, realistic, or entirely improbable. If you are already enjoying fantasizing, but are more frequently not involving your partner, you are still in a positive place... a private playground with a variety of mental play. When you are ready, begin introducing your partner to these scenarios to associate pleasurable feelings with your partner. Bring them in for a cameo appearance at first, and don't be disappointed if on the first few attempts, it doesn't take. When you use visualization, you are reprogramming your conditioned response. If you fantasize about people other than your partner, you are in the majority; in a study conducted amongst heterosexual university students and employees who were currently in committed relationships, 98% of men and 80% of women reported that they occasionally fantasize about people other than their partners (Leitenberg & Hicks, 2001.) Although this study was limited, there is nothing to suggest that you should feel guilty about having private sexual fantasies about others. Use what already excites you to bring you closer to building exciting sexual fantasies involving your partner.

When it comes to sharing your fantasies with your partner, you should exercise some caution and judgment in order to minimize misunderstandings. The goal is to enhance your sexual experience, not offend or make one another uncomfortable. There are a few guidelines for having this conversation with your partner.

Although most people don't fantasize about their partner all the time, be extremely careful with sharing any fantasies with them that involve others as it can easily hurt their feelings. Hence, it is important to genuinely try to integrate them into your own daydreaming before you broach this topic.

- Remember that most fantasies are not to be taken literally, but instead be interpreted symbolically. Fantasies are not expectations but fun ideas; play with them as precursors to realistic sexual acts.

- Use this conversation to share what turns you on, and to learn more about what excites your partner. Your willingness to share will hopefully give your partner the comfort they need to similarly open up with you.

- Remember that your partner wants to feel and see you excited as much as you want to bring them pleasure.

- Not all fantasies involve others but are less direct or fetishes on ideas, objects, garments, specific body parts.

A couple real examples: I once was in a long term relationship with a man who loved the feel of satin against his skin under the belt. He wasn't interested in wearing it but loved the implication that it was used in women's lingerie. He was over the moon when

I purchased a silky negligee that we use to stimulate him after he shared this fantasy with me. We shared a few giggles at first but it playing along and indulging him made him so comfortable and free to talk about and try several other ideas… and they were all fun!

Another man I loved, who was seemingly sexually repressed, slowly revealed to me he was excited by women's feet. This admission was made after a few observations of his behavior on my part: he was very eager to rub my feet and hold them. After telling him how much I enjoyed the attention he was giving me, I asked him why he commonly gravitated to my feet, and he blushed and told me he thought they were soft and pretty, and that he really enjoyed touching them. It took a few weeks for the full admission to be revealed that he was sexually aroused by touching women's feet, and I welcomed it with enthusiasm. I would invite him to touch them or send him photos of my toes in pretty shoes, giving him permission to enjoy a fantasy he was so concerned would trouble me. My enabling him to indulge in an entirely harmless fantasy brought him a much needed sexual liberation that opened us up to a number of fun sexual experiences, and truly broadened my own sexual repertoire.

Fantasies involving other people are the tricky ones. Commonly one partner or another may be excited by the idea of a threesome or group sex. I am definitely not opposed to the healthy expression of this fantasy but if your partner admits this, don't feel that you have to directly act it out. As before, sometimes a fantasy is just mental fiction that gets us excited. However open minded you may be, I wouldn't recommend blazing this trail if you as a couple are already experiencing problems. You want to rebuild the passion in your shared relationship, and bringing another person into the mix will provide novelty but most definitely not fix any of the underlying issues that are creating difficulties in your sex life. It will do more damage than good and runs the risk of one of you taking it as permission to look elsewhere for sexual satisfaction. I believe that multiple partner sex acts are for firmly established couples, swingers, or unattached individuals. A fun exercise to try is to simulate the fantasy via toys and props. Without being too explicit, I would recommend small vibrators for men who are bisexual and or/strap on dildos for the women who partner with them. If you are in a lesbian or bisexual relationship with a woman, the same toys are good suggestions. In a cisgender straight relationship you can simulate a threesome by introducing a penetration toy such as a silicone sheath toy which your partner can use while you think of other creative ways to stimulate him. There are some very creative versions available ranging from realistic to "nonthreatening" and simple products. Blindfolds or a darkened setting can help the fantasy along by reducing visual stimuli, allowing your partner to feel closer to the fantasy in their minds.

Role playing, as corny as it sounds, can be very successful when indulging a partner's (or your own) fantasy of new partners. No one is telling you to dress up in a naughty nurse outfit and demand he take his medicine orally… but a more subtle version of role play is a good place to start. You can tease and encourage verbally by saying things which are uncharacteristic to you. Another fun trick is if you are educated in a foreign language… try that for good measure. One can jokingly try out these elements interspersed with more traditional sex.

A couple caveats to the types of role playing that should not be attempted by beginners: rape role plays as well as bondage and discipline scenarios. Both of these simulate acts and scenarios in which there is a huge margin of error and the fun can end really quickly if one of you becomes uncomfortable. They involve trust, comfort, and some level of prework in the form of defining limits and communication. Another important thing to remember when experimenting with role playing is to be very clear at the onset that it is pretend. You don't want to confuse your partner, and you want to be certain that they are ok with it.

With role playing, you have the opportunity to toss aside your traditions, shake up expectations, and try something new under the guise of assuming a different personality. You may find there are elements that you can assume into your own sexual identity that enhance your experience.

CHAPTER 13

WHEN TO USE PORNOGRAPHY

This topic ties in neatly with using fantasizing to reignite your love life. Before you use pornography as a tool, you should likely first explore sharing mutual fantasies. Many people find pornography distasteful or are uncomfortable with the taboo of it. Many believe that pornography is destructive for couples and encourages cheating or polyamory. Others find the idealistic images of human attractiveness to be damaging to self confidence and detrimental to body image. All of this has a ring of truth to it for certain scenarios and specific types of pornography. The tricky part is finding body-positive, couple friendly, fun, loving, healthy sexual representation via images and video. You may be surprised at the ubiquity of pornography and the ease in which it can be accessed, however the positive spin is that with that ubiquity, an increasing amount of female-friendly and couple-friendly content is out there. If you are willing to experiment with what works for you, and be brave about searching, you're on the right track.

Despite all the bad press about porn, numerous couples' counselors recommend the use of pornography to spice things up in an otherwise waning sex life. A better name for this "tasteful" type of sexual imagery is erotica. Combined with you and your partners own masturbatory imagery, you can add to the sexual scenarios that turn you on. An additional benefit of utilizing pornography and erotic content is that since the majority of women require more foreplay and build up prior to sexual intercourse than men, pornography is a fun way to get you physically and mentally prepared to be close to your male partner (particularly if male stamina is a challenge for your relationship.)

However, it is important to better understand your partner's preferences and boundaries before viewing any form of pornography together; as is can easily backfire on you. Unfortunately, there are far too many films and images that can be perceived as violent or emotionally harmful, and as an adult couple, you can choose to avoid these media portrayals. Before you venture into this territory, understand what you and your partner find offensive, distasteful, upsetting, or unattractive and avoid pornography that includes these elements. However, ensure that you are also viewing images and scenarios that excite you. Here is another area in which your closeness and sense of humor can bridge initial awkwardness. You have to be prepared to endure some of the inherent ridiculousness of pornography, giggle through it, but be able to sustain your disbelief enough to enjoy it for what it is; a fantasy. If this is a first for you and your partner, be extremely cautious with your selection, and make it very apparent that you can end the experience at any time. One suggestion is to be silly and and enact some of the over-dramatized expressions of arousal you are viewing. Chances are in your play, you may find the pressure of the moment comes away from both of you and you may find yourselves upstaging the actors on screen.

CHAPTER 14

PLASTIC THINGS THAT BUZZ

Now that we've explored the potentials of fantasizing and erotica, let's broach another topic you may or may not find intimidating: sex toys. Do you own one? You should. If you do not already own a sex toy (or toys) it is totally worth your investment. There are varying styles, types, and qualities, of course, but if you are unsure what you will like, start with the basics: A smaller more stylized vibrator (shaped more like a rocket or bullet rather than a penis or with protrusions), cock rings, cock rings with small vibrators, tingling cream, light bondage (silk restraints, blindfolds, etc.) Introducing a toy / accessory into your sexual routine is a great way to transfer the pressure away from your partner's performance and ego. It's also super hot to watch you or your partner pleasure oneself or the other with a toy as you can be an observer and a participant at your will. If you have never tried a vibrator before, I recommend getting used to it solo before you bring it into partner sex. It's important to know how and if it will please you before you bring in the added pressure of having your partner present and / or using the toy on you. I also recommend using it alone until you know how or if it can bring you to orgasm before you introduce it to the bedroom; this will give you confidence in your ability to climax and in your libido, will get you familiar with the toy and how it works, and will give you assurance you still can have an orgasm. Vibrators can be a girl's best friend in and out of partner sex. If you are having difficulty reaching orgasm in general using a vibrator is a great way to retrain your ability to reach climax alone so that you can more easily recognize when you may reach climax with your partner. It will help you recognize the patterns and pressure that work for you rather than testing it out in a scenario in which another person's ego is involved along with your own.

If male performance is an issue with your sex life, it is first and foremost a sensitive topic for both of you. Exercise caution when approaching this topic; and be sensitive. If an issue with your male partner is that he climaxes sooner than you would like, a penis ring could be a fun option for both of you. A penis ring is typically made of silicone or a stretchy plastic that is pushed down over the shaft and down to the base of the penis to restrict the blood flow out of the penis once it fills the blood vessels and creates turgidity. It keeps him from softening as easily and can also delay climax so that you may enjoy intercourse and sexual activity longer and at a pace and pressure that you need longer yet may not otherwise be tolerate by his reflexes without some assistance. Penis rings come in many styles and variations, some which boast miniature stimulators for a female partner at the base, some which have a loop for or girth to accommodate the testicles, some with varied texture, and others with varied stiffness. A couple important points in properly using a penis ring is that the fit is firm yet not uncomfortable, and should only be worn for up to 20 - 30 minutes at a time. You want your lover to have a positive experience, and for you to know he is safe and comfortable. Chances are your lover will enjoy the extended performance provided by the ring and will help build confidence in his abilities to please you sexually. If you want to continue using this option, make sure to share with him that you enjoyed it and why so that he is aware that it pleases you and brings you closer. Other toys that are useful are ben wa balls for toning and tightening the female pelvic muscles. Women claim that using the balls for a few minutes a day create stimulation and provide kegel muscle toning which contributes to an enhanced sexual pleasure for women and their male partners. However, you can perform these exercises without the ben wa balls but it will require a more conscious effort. It is purported that kegel exercises can also provide women with stronger orgasms. I say it's worth a try! Another important message to you is: don't forget the lube. There are myriad types of lubricant available to us that can help improve and make sex more comfortable. My personal favorites are warming lubricant and silicone lubricant. Different lubes are available for different sex acts as well. Some are great for couples who like to intersperse oral sex in their routine, others are wonderful for use with toys, and many are made with female pleasure and intensity in mind. This is another easy way to introduce sex toys and products into your bedroom. If you aren't already a lube convert, you should take yourself to the nearest drugstore and pick some up tonight. First always test a product on your skin to ensure you will not have any reaction to the ingredients. Then you can use it with your partner, and use it again and again. I hope you run out of it quickly!

CHAPTER 15

MIND YOUR MANNERS

Most of us when we start dating are on our best behavior. We use grateful and polite language, respectful gestures, we excuse ourselves and / or are very private about bodily functions, we eat politely, and we express interest in one another's lives and activities. We are clean, kind, considerate, and seek to make our partners feel comfortable before ourselves. As time wears on, it also wears on our manners. Being comfortable in our own skins and in our own homes and lives is one of the nicest aspects of a long-standing relationship. Inevitably, we will slip up, and often times we can laugh about it. When we find ourselves annoyed with one another and the patterns that we can fall into, that is where it can seriously erode sexual attraction. Having lived with my partner for some time now, I struggled with being so perpetually annoyed with his noisiness that I found it prevented me from finding him sexually attractive. He felt more like an obnoxious older brother than my live-in boyfriend, and I was repulsed by him. He picked up on my lack of sexual interest and asked me why I wasn't responding to his advances or making any of my own volition. I asked him if he was truly ready to have a discussion about it or if he wanted to set aside time later. He was in fact in a great position to have an adult conversation and I shared with him that I wasn't used to living with someone, let alone someone so different than me. I shared with him that I knew he was unaware of how much it bothered me but the noisy way he went about his day left my nerves frazzled by the end of the day which sapped my ability to find him cute or sexy. I politely provided examples of behaviors which could be altered to improve my mood; gently closing cabinets and doors, speaking more softly. Since this conversation he has made several improvements to his manners in being respectful of my presence in the house and because I am far less annoyed with him, we have a lot more sex! This was perfect motivation for the preferred behavior.

Now step back for a moment and reflect on your current behavior in the relationship and compare it to how you acted in the beginning. Are you behaving much differently? Spend some time considering what typed of reactions your partner displays in regards to these behaviors; do you notice avoidance or irritability? If you want him to improve his manners and behavior, you'll need to be willing to honestly evaluate your own and make changes as well.

My grandparents and parents were incredible to each other in this regard; they were great examples of how to be respectful and polite to one another but not stiff and stuffy about it. Even after decades of marriage, they were quick to thank one another, open doors, and do kind things to let one another know how much they were appreciated. The effect is a reciprocal cycle of kindness and respect, which I believe is one of the secrets to longevity in love. If you and your partner have fallen out of good habits with one another, try to be as polite as possible around and to your partner; it may freak them out at first and they'll feel like you are acting strangely but the fun part is watching how their behavior changes as a result. It puts in stark contrast how we can fall into habits of taking each other's kindness and consideration for granted.

Whether or not my partner has polite eating habits is on my deal breaker list. I have broken up with men because they chew with their mouth open, are rude at the table, etc. Not only is it rude, but it's completely unsexy and disgusting. What are your eating habits like? What are your partner's eating habits like? This can be a big one because you may be so used to doing things a certain way and may be completely unaware that what you are doing grosses out your partner. You wouldn't go out for buffalo wings, corn on the cob and crab legs on a first date, would you? I'd bet that most of you would say "hell no!" I can assume that would be less worry about staining your clothing than it is risking grossing out your partner. As we get closer, we can enjoy these types of foods together, and we get comfortable seeing one another chow down and get messy. It can be fun and silly, of course, but consider how you eat and how you behave at the table in front of your partner. Is it unsavory? You can still enjoy your food and be polite at the same time. If you are struggling with your partner's manners in this regard, there are ways to express to them it bothers you to see them behave that way. Behavior is best corrected as it is occurring. Some great examples of ways to correct table manners (and any bad manners for that matter) can be phrased something like "I've noticed you don't place your napkin in your lap when you eat, why is that?" or, "You probably don't realize this, but you chew with your mouth open sometimes and I find it very distracting." My personal experience in managing these types of scenarios is also opening the door to my partner to share with me if there is something I'm doing that may bother him. A great way to frame it is, "I hope that we're close enough so that you can tell me anything about myself that you think I should know." He might not tell you then and there that you make him upset or he prefers other behaviors, but he'll let you know later.

Here's another big one: cell phone use. Of course, we are all guilty of this at some point but one of the biggest modern complaints when it comes to manners is inappropriate use of cell phones around our partners. Have you seen couples at a restaurant sitting together but both on their phones? How does that make you feel about the state of their relationship? We have our cell phones glued to or bodies like another appendage it seems, and they are so vital to the speed and level of connectedness we need to keep up with modern life. However the very thing we believe keeps us connected can erode our most precious relationships. Think about how you would have acted on your first date with your partner; would you have pulled out your phone and taken a call? Would you have checked facebook or texted your friends during dinner or in front of him? (If the answer is yes, there is a much bigger problem to solve.) Most of us would answer, "absolutely not!" So why is it that we do it as we get more comfortable in our partnerships? As ubiquitous as they are, it is still incredibly rude to be on your phone when you are supposed to be spending time with your loved one. When you pick up the phone or he picks up the phone the message it sends is that the person or thing on the other end is more important than the person in front of you or them, or that they would rather be talking to another person. Don't answer your phone, unless you absolutely have to. If you are expecting an important call or message from work or someone you care about, preface it with your partner and ask that they do the same for you. You want to know if there are any exceptions for the time you are spending together, and you can rest assured that when he checks his phone or when you do that it is only for that purpose. Another way to navigate the necessary phone check is to keep it short and to ask permission to take the call. Rarely anyone will say no but just the act of acknowledging the necessity of it reassures your partner and reassures you that it is important but will be brief and then you can focus on the other person again. Never check your email at the table or play on facebook when you are supposed to be with your partner. And please… please… don't take pictures of your food at a nice restaurant. First of all, no one needs to see what you are eating, it serves no purpose and it is definitely not more important than the impression you will make if you are rude at the table. Ideally, your cell phone should be off or on silent when you are scheduled to spend time with someone, especially your lover. My boyfriend and I agree on the cell phone policy and he likes to joke with people who do it, "If it's not on facebook / instagram / twitter, it didn't happen?!?" If you have to take that call, excuse yourself, explain the nature of the call and walk away from the table.

CHAPTER 16

THE ART OF FLIRTING

No matter where you are in your relationship we all like to be flirted with. Have you ever been in a relationship for a while and you find yourself flattered by the small flirtations of waiters, the person on the subway, the man who you pass in the grocery store? It feels good doesn't it? And then we begin to compare our current relationships with these strangers who made us feel good for a few moments. It is likely because there is very little flirting in your own relationship. We take for granted the subtle art of flirting with the people to whom we are attracted. Flirting is especially a great way for couples who have very little time or privacy to have sex, express their desire for one another. Finding ways to communicate desire to your partner via flirting is shorthand for saying, "I find you desirable, I love you, and if I could, I would make love to you right now." All flirting is not a lead in to sex, but an expression of intimacy and desire, essential things to bringing more fire into your relationship. However when we are in a long standing relationship we are often worried that all flirting will be taken as a guarantee that we will have sex. As much as a surprise as it is for some, all flirting doesn't have to lead to sex and can be satisfying in its own right. We can stop flirting with one another because of this reason, particularly women who have very little energy left or very limited privacy. As women, our one of our primary sexual organs is our brain. When we want to get in the mood, we need the mental foreplay of flirting. If you stop flirting and playing throughout the day it becomes very difficult for women to have positive and fulfilling sexual experiences with our partners. To reintroduce a culture of flirting in your relationship you may need to be the first mover, the initiator. Flirting is such a playful and effective way to communicate desire and acknowledge your partner's desire. Here are a few tips for amping up your partner flirting:

- Sexy emails or texts: because it is something that someone else may see, keep it sweet and fun, rather than pornographic unless you know the other person is in a position to enjoy it. Surprise one another; that's the important part.

- Eye contact and pointed smiles are the fundamentals of flirting. If you are at a party or an event with other people, make him feel like he's the only one in the room by giving him your sexiest smile and attention. Do it at home, on the bus, touch his leg in the car, let him hear you talk about how wonderful he is, and make sure he knows it's meant more for his ears than others.

- When talking with him, make excuses to touch him; put your hand on his chest or arm. Walk closely to him. Or when you pass by, graze and hand along his neck or back.

- Another fun way is to play footsie with him under the table. It doesn't have to be full blown rubbing, but as simple as touching and not moving away, confirming your comfort with his body and his company.

CHAPTER 17

LEAVE LOVE NOTES

There are so many ways this can work to your advantage, and is by far one of my favorite standbys when I feel that my partner needs an extra boost or a reminder that he is desired, loved, and wanted. My partner and I travel often and he always wakes up earlier than I do as I am a night owl. I want to make sure he's reminded that even though I am not with him that he knows I am thinking of him and want him close. I sneak notes into his briefcase after he goes to bed, I set them on the nightstand, I put them on his mirror, I leave them in his blazer pockets, some to be seen immediately, and some to be found later. It doesn't even have to be something poetic or incredibly lyrical, just a simple "I'm thinking about you!" or "you are my best friend and lover," even something as goofy as a little doodle with some intention to show I care. He appreciates these so much and they often prompt the cutest calls or messages when he finds them.

My habit of doing this for him has got him started leaving me similar messages around the house. We even have a silly tradition of moving around a stuffed squirrel toy and putting it in silly scenarios such as making coffee or stealing the remote control. It makes us giggle and is a bit of an inside joke. Oftentimes the squirrel delivers love notes – primarily the humorous ones. One time I thumbed a heart and our initials in the dirt in his car, or left a message on the shower door so that when it steamed up he could see the writing. There are so many ways to leave a sweet or silly message that can cheer up your lover and remind them that they are your number one priority.

CHAPTER 18

TAKE A BREAK FROM EACH OTHER

Every couple needs time apart. Newly blossoming lovers often spend every waking minute together, but eventually, they need a bit of space and distance to stay sane. But do you recall what if felt like to return home and see your partner after a time apart? Or how you felt when they greeted you with a huge hug and eagerness on your return? Time apart gives all of us the opportunity to miss one another and let go of some of the little things that nag at us through day to day life. Before you can want to come back together, you need to be separate for a while; fire needs air. My boyfriend and I have very different interests and activities that we care about but we are also quite independent people and often do things without one another and take trips apart. I find that this is one of the secrets of our longevity, and keeps us from getting frustrated with one another. One of the keys to a sweet return is to ensure your partner that there is no alternate motive for leaving without him other than your own well being and pleasure. Take a kinking trip with your girlfriends or go take a spa weekend alone and recharge. Encourage him to do the same. Make sure that the other partner is aware of what you are doing and where you are but avoid constant contact or you will not realize the benefits of time apart and getting a breather from your life with your partner. I find that when we return to one another we are grateful for one another's company, have new things to talk about and are both refreshed and happy to see each other. If you aren't able to take a few days, even an afternoon or a full day apart can work wonders. Set the expectation that you are going to be out of contact for a while and then stick to it. You are both unique human beings with unique needs and experiences, and it is one of the reasons why you fell in love in the first place. If you aren't pursuing unique experiences and doing things that interest you because your partner isn't keen on them, you will feel resentment and inevitably the two of you will get bored with one another. This translates into the bedroom as well. We are attracted to people whom we find fascinating and admirable. Our independent experiences and desires shape who we are and how others view us. So go out there, Let have a great time, and encourage your lover to do the same. Give yourselves time to actually miss one other for a change. Too much closeness can stifle desire. There is a difference between interest and closeness and what can be perceived as surveillance and suspicion. Time apart allows us to focus on what is truly important as well as providing relief from routine and expectations of being together. Make a conscious effort to incorporate space into your relationship to heat things up again, even though it may be uncomfortable at first.

CHAPTER 19

WORKING AROUND YOUR "LITTLE PARTY CRASHERS"

All of these tips seem doable for single couples, but what about those of your with young children. On top of the possibility of you both having careers and commitments, along with the laundry list of chares and the mile long to do lists involved in managing your life and those in your family, the idea of sex and intimacy seems as likely that you would win the lottery or find a giraffe grazing in your back yard. Here is where some careful planning needs to come in to play. You may need to sacrifice the thrill of spontaneity of time and place so that the two of you are on the same plane when it comes time to get sexy. You need to make time for sex and time alone as much as you need to plan the numerous appointments and activities to keep your family healthy and fed. Happy children have happy parents, and they pick up when their parents aren't in love anymore or if there is tension or resentment. You need to come to an agreement with your partner to make time to be sexual a habit like all the other things that are healthy and good in life. The idea of scheduled sex may be unappealing to you or your partner but there are other ways to frame it in your mind. The anticipation and expectation may be even better for female partners who need more time and preparation to get in the mood. A way to think of it as an analogy is to recall how you feel when you know you will be dining at a favorite restaurant, you know the menu is good and there are definite favorites and standbys if the specials aren't to your taste. Also, with the expectation and regularity, it may open the doors to trying something new because you have a pattern of intimacy and if it doesn't work this time, you can go to your favorite dishes.

However you need to be ready to pounce on the moments and opportunities that present themselves to you as rare as they can be when you are parents. You've got to take time to remind yourselves why you entered into this beautiful chaotic mess that is parenting in the first place. You behaviors don't even need to be overtly sexual; it can be as simple as holding hands walking or spontaneously dancing to piped music in the store, a quick make out session in the bathroom, but you can't make it wait until your scheduled time either. Don't postpone intimate expression if the timing isn't perfect you can find ways to connect with one another along the way and in between. Couples with young children will admit to you that they have mastered the art of the quickie. Granted, for us women, it often isn't as pleasing as longer sexual encounters, but it gets you primed for the next time and helps you feel more connected to your partner. Particularly when you are loathe leaving your children alone or unobserved for even short periods of time. Understand when you can actually close the door and steal a few minutes together.

New parents should revisit what they define as intimacy. It doesn't have to be intercourse. And new mothers experience hormonal and physical changes that make sex the very last thing on their minds. It is important that the other parent understands this before hand and that you make time to talk about this post partum as well. All sexual activity doesn't have to end in orgasm, remember that. And there are many sexual activities that are safe and comfortable for new mothers. Remind yourselves that you are not just parents, and that you are independent human beings with needs and desires equally important. Honor you and your partners needs as much as those of your children and you'll keep the door open for intimacy and passion.

CHAPTER 20

TAKE A PERSONALITY TEST

A great tool to promote deeper understanding between you and your partner is a valid personality test. Many of you have heard of the Myers-Briggs Type Indicator, a validated and very accurate assessment that gives insight into four foundational personality traits which are patterns in our ways of perceiving and reacting to the world around us. All of the sixteen type combinations are of equal value and there is no one bad personality type among them.

"When you understand personality preferences, you can more readily appreciate differences between you and people closest to you, such as spouses, partners, children, and friends. In most areas of life, when differences between you and another person are bothersome, you can avoid the other person in some way. But when that person is a loved one or close friend, you have a lot to lose by walking away. Knowledge of personality type allows you to see those differences as just those—different ways of "being." Instead of labeling a person and putting value judgments on his or her behavior, you can learn to see it as behavior reflecting personality type, not something designed to offend you. Many couples learn to appreciate these differences and may even see them in a humorous light." (http://www.myersbriggs.org)

There are many resources available to help you interpret the interactions between your type and your partner's type and how to create a relationship environment that is best suited to both of you. It can help you both feel closer to one another and consider new ways to connect.

Another useful assessment to try is the Mayer-Salovey-Caruso Emotional Intelligence Test (or MSCEIT.) The term "emotional intelligence" means an intelligence having to do with emotions consisting of two parts: emotion and intelligence. In the context of this test, emotions refer to the feelings and reactions a person has, which can be in response to a real or an imagined relationship. Intelligence, in this context, refers to the ability to reason with or about something. The concept of emotional intelligence is referring to how a person reasons with their emotions, or conversely, how emotions assist a person's thinking. The MSCEIT measures the capacity to reason with emotions and emotional signals, as well as the capacity of emotion to enhance thought. Another easy resource to use for measuring and understanding emotional Intelligence is the book, Emotional Intelligence 2.0 by Travis Bradberry and Jean Graves. The book describes how a person can improve and understand self-awareness, self-management, social awareness, and relationship management in context of emotional intelligence.

With these tools in mind, it may be very useful for you to understand your own as well as your partner's capacity in this respect.

CHAPTER 21

KEEPING THE MYSTERY ALIVE

Sometimes we confuse intimacy with sharing every detail of our lives. Contrary to this belief, your partner does not need to know everything about you to experience intimacy as a couple. Sharing more of yourself with your partner than others does indeed produce a feeling of deep connection, however, divulging every little detail can be too much information. Keep in mind that a little bit of mystery helps your relationship. Naturally, this doesn't mean you should withhold from your partner on purpose or not share your feelings, but it means can make a choice to consciously decide what to share, and what to keep to yourself. One thing that is not intended by keeping the mystery alive is to never act aloof. Mystery isn't withholding or deceit, or hiding important parts of you in order to be appealing. This can cause suspicion and tension with your partner. Know the difference between the essentials and the things that can be kept to yourself. It's not also what you verbally share but what you allow each other to see. Living together or spending a great amount of time with one another can get you both in a position where you are over sharing. Do you use the toilet with the door open, shave your legs in front of him, clip your toenails while having a conversation? (This idea ties into the manners section as well!) There's something to be said for the magic of transformation in our beauty rituals, the privacy we liked to have in the beginning of the relationship. One trick I like to use often is to not allow my partner to see me naked for a while. It drives him crazy. By getting dressed and toweling off privately, not bopping around the house naked, he has to use his imagination. There can be such thing as too much of a good thing; being naked gets you both too used to one another's bodies and can strip away all the eroticism (pun intended.)

A more modern problem with over sharing is on social media. Over sharing on facebook or twitter (etc.) can be especially hazardous for couples. Broadcasting details of your relationship, positive or negative, can be very unhealthy. Some people really don't like everyone knowing things about their private life, happy moments included. Negative posts or comments, or even some that may appear harmless can come across as you or your partner criticizing one another. When it's out there for everyone to see, you have the added factor of humiliation or embarrassment to you and your partner. Also, if the two of you follow one another on any of these platforms, and you both post everything, what is there for you to talk about at the end of the day? A healthy relationship requires spending time together in person. Part of intimacy is privacy; those beautiful moments you share still happened even if no one else reads about it. Keeping special things just between the two of you creates a bond.

Having separate social lives is also part of remaining interesting and captivation to your partner. Unique interests and experiences are part of the amazing people we are and those with whom we fall in love.

CHAPTER 22

SURPRISE!

There's something delightful about pleasant surprises for your partner; do something out of the norm yet positive for them like taking a day off of work and taking a day trip. You've got to be mindful of your partner's obligations and schedules before you do something out of the blue, or they can backfire. Coming up with fun and loving surprises can really stump you if you aren't used to doing something like that. Here are a few ideas that may work:

- Have the bar play his favorite song or raise a toast to him just because.

- Call him in the middle of the day and say "Hi. I love you, and there is carrot cake in the fridge."

- Fill his closet with balloons

- Prepare an impromptu picnic

- Get his friends to "kidnap" him and take him to a surprise date with you

- Pick him up from the airport with nothing but underwear under your long coat

- Set up a treasure hunt in your home with a treat or an indication that you are the treat!

A little bit of planning goes a long way to show your partner that you care and that they are special to you, in your thoughts and worthy of your attention.

CHAPTER 23

TAKE A TECHNOLOGY DIET

The average American adult watches about 35 hours of television a week (that's about 5 hours of TV a day.) This is not counting the time we spend on the internet, on our smart phones, listening to the radio, or time spent on other mobile devices for other purposes besides viewership. Granted, senior citizens are those who spend the most time watching TV, the hours increase as we age, so depending on your age group, the US averages are below (Nielson "Cross-Platform Report" March 2014):

- 2-11 years: 24 hours, 16 minutes
- 12-17 years: 20 hours, 41 minutes
- 18-24 years: 22 hours, 27 minutes
- 25-34 years: 27 hours, 36 minutes

- 35-49 years: 33 hours, 40 minutes
- 50-64 years: 43 hours, 56 minutes
- 65-plus years: 50 hours, 34 minutes

The statistics are a bit surprising, and it's eye opening to realize that if you cut down the time you spend looking at screens each day, you could have better relationships with the people you love. We often lament that we don't have enough time anymore. Take a close look at how you are spending your time; how much of you and your partner's time is spent watching TV or using mobile devices for viewership? It is typical to want to turn off our active thinking and relax in front of the TV for a while; and you should feel comfortable doing this when you need to or when there is something on in which you are deeply interested. However, determine whether you are watching TV because you care about the program, or if you are just flipping though to see what is on. I'm not a big fan of regular TV programming and so this is easier for me, I typically watch a few programs, those I can procure via movie services or online and watch when my schedule permits. Technology has made it nearly impossible to miss our favorite shows: we can stream what we like and care about when it is convenient for us, rather than scheduled time and commercial breaks. Take advantage of this and be sure to not neglect your partner, or allow your partner to neglect you because of the tube. A way to introduce this to your partner is by asking for more time together, then point out that you believe it is possible if the two of you cut out a certain number of hours of media viewership a week, pledge that time to him / her as well so that both of you are committed to spending less time in front of the TV or on your media devices.

A couple other tips to remove temptation is to power off or to silence mobile devices after a specific hour. Either that or put them in a different room so that you can only check them when you purposefully do so and when you need to rather than casually or habitually. If you have a television in your bedroom, take it out today. Put it somewhere else as soon as possible. Having a TV in the room in which you sleep and rest is bad sleep hygiene, first and foremost, because it prevents us from falling asleep at proper times, disrupts our normal sleep cycles, and prevents us from having quality rest. We also don't need our last conscious thoughts each day to be dictated by something outside of ourselves. Secondly, if you live with your partner, you should spend the time in the bedroom with nothing interfering between time to wind down, rest, read, cuddle, sleep, and have sex. The evening is a very important time for busy couples to reconnect and have close conversations. If there is a TV or mobile device in your bedroom, these connecting and intimate conversations are less likely to happen and will undoubtedly happen less frequently. Studies also indicate that couples with TVs in their bedrooms have nearly half as much sex as those who do not. If the idea of boycotting all media in your bedroom is daunting, try it for a month or a few weeks. Be mindful of how the absence of TV, mobile devices, and work materials from your bedroom affects your relationship.

CHAPTER 24

BENEFITS OF COUNSELING

It's difficult to know when it is time to seek counseling for sexual difficulty. It can be intimidating and frightening to talk about your intimacy with your partner, in front of your partner, and to a third party. It's important to consider when you would opt to visit a professional, and at what point do you go? How can simply talking about it improve your sex life? During sex therapy, you talk about sex with your partner and the therapist, and the therapist is trained in and comfortable with talking about sex. However, getting started can be the hardest part. While during your session, nothing is too taboo to talk about with your therapist, couples oftentimes find it nearly impossible to start talking. A sex therapist is aware of the anxiety and hesitation you and your partner may feel at the onset and is prepared to coach and guide the two of you progressively. This type of therapy can get to the root of the problem; couples often find themselves at an impasse because anger, inhibition, pain, resentment, or accusations and or assumptions can prevent the necessary discussions to occur. Most couples who have issues do so because they have put off talking about them together for so long that the issues become complicated with these intense feelings, and the patterns of negative behavior become stronger and more solidified. The fear of confronting the issue and the fear that you may discover the two of you are incompatible that you can delay the necessary discussions.

What typically happens when you visit a sex therapist? You go as a couple, you will likely be asked to fill out questionnaires regarding your sexual orientation, history, upbringing, what you are hurting about, sexual preferences, comfort level with different sexual activities, and medical information. Some therapists like to do separate interviews as well. The therapist will analyze responses from the two of you and build a roadmap for therapy based on the findings. Reading and content is often recommended, and at times touching and activities are suggested to the couple. The therapy is conducted in a way that neither partner feels as though they have to submit to the demands of the other, however, in some instances, compromises are suggested to permit progress. The goal is to ensure neither partner feels that they have to give up too much of what they want and need to be sexually happy in the relationship.

The most common problems brought to sex therapists are those related to low sexual desire and disagreements about frequency of sex. According to a Psychology Today article, "Women who don't have orgasms and men who ejaculate too quickly are often the quickest problems to solve – no pun intended. Erectile dysfunction and ejaculating too slowly are other male problems my clinic works with. Breast cancer and prostate cancer survivors should receive mandatory sex therapy as part of their recovery. Technique problems, issues with oral sex, "ick" factor feelings about different sex acts, problems with porn, boring sex lives, can't get aroused, can't tell your partner to brush his teeth, inhibitions, suspected addictions and fetishes are common reasons to seek a sex therapist."

How long does sex therapy take to show results? As many things, it varies. Some things are quick fixes and others are months of work, particularly those which are tied up in a power struggle in the relationship. Sometimes other forms of couples counseling are employed to fix deeper rooted issues. Sexual issues rooted in trauma or abuse can take years to resolve; if you discover that you or your partner have sexual issues related to trauma or abuse, practice the utmost patience and understanding with each other... and yourself.

It's ok if talking about sex to your therapist occasionally arouses you. Your therapist is trained in balancing approachability and professionalism required and they are aware that intimate conversations can stir feelings and responses in us. Your therapist has firm ethical boundaries about the client / therapist relationship that should keep you comfortable and safe when discussing your feelings and responses.

Other tips on entering into a therapeutic treatment with your partner include:

- Understanding that the issues likely won't resolve immediately

- Take time for reflection

- Make sure you use language that lets your partner know that you have heard them, don't be silent as it can be confused with anger or disapproval.

- Refuse to impose generalities on one another; consider what is unique about what your partner is saying to you.

- Remember that the goal is mutual happiness

- Avoid making judgments: your partner is at their most vulnerable sharing fantasies and / or fears. Keep a mindset and a language of acceptance

- Try to focus on the common ground; often there are enjoyable alternatives for something which feels like a roadblock.

CHAPTER 25

ORGANIZE A "SEXUAL RETREAT"

Plan Friday night through Sunday Evening to be just you and your partner. Even in our busy lifestyle, you can make this happen, with some good planning and a healthy mindset. The ground rules are: No kids, no phones, no emails, no computers, no work…just you and your partner. If you can go to a place away from the home, this is highly recommended so that you won't be tempted by any distractions. Here's the agenda:

Friday Night:

The goal is to be relaxed and peaceful. Eat dinner together and consciously try not to talk about, kids, bills, work, or negative world events. Consume alcohol in moderation, set limits on consumption.

Saturday:

Focus on understanding each other's arousal patterns and how certain touches can have more of an effect later on in the contact / foreplay. An exercise is for each partner to take turns rating the intensity of feeling associated with partner touches. A numerical scale of 1-5 is easy for you and your partner to gauge intensity rather than simply saying, "That's nice, I like that." Start with neutral spots on your body and progress to the more erogenous zones. Later in the day a great activity is to independently evaluate your sexual patterns in writing. Some great ones are:

1. "In my opinion, our weaknesses regarding sexual intimacy are........."
2. "My contributions to the difficulties are........."
3. "One specific, concrete thing, I need from you to make this better is........."
4. "From my end, I commit to making things even better by........."

You can also write down specific, concrete requests such as, "Tell me 3 things you like about my body?" or "I would love if you would give me a backrub before sex."

Take a walk or exercise after this exercise to clear your mind and activate your body.

Plan to have a snack and a light drink.

Set aside time to make love or experience intimate touching or a shared bath.

Enjoy dinner out with no expectations to make love after. Rest well in whatever way works best for you both.

Sunday:

Focus on broadening your sexual repertoire. There are some tips to expanding it:

Verbally share with your partner a fantasized fast and a fantasized slow encounter with one another.

You can practice "edging" in which you bring yourself and your partner close to orgasm and then stop. Relax, and then begin again. The third time, allow orgasm. This technique helps increase the intensity of orgasm in both women and men.

Independently brainstorm a list of all the sex acts you can think of in ten minutes without judgment of you or your partner. Once complete, select two ideas from your list that are new and that you are willing to try and do one or more! Another version and / or option is to repeat this exercise with positions. Make it a point to do everything out of the norm. Make time to make love in a new way today.

The idea of the sex retreat isn't a good idea for couples who frequently fight over sex. You should enter into this in the instance in which you believe a concentrated effort from both of you would be accepted and welcomed.

The time alone together should be positive in and of itself even if you can't make it through some of the activities. Also remember to take a few hours to yourself to reflect and to relax alone.

CHAPTER 26

THE MYSTERIOUS FEMALE ORGASM

From a personal perspective I find that the topic of the realistic expectations of female orgasm to be one of high importance. Even very sexually experienced men and women can harbor belief in the myths of how often, how quickly, and how important orgasming is to women in partnered relationships. Very few women expect to or want to go through the effort it takes to orgasm every time they have sex with their partner. When women do, we can oftentimes judge ourselves negatively, specifically heterosexual women, in comparison with our male partners. Women can experience anxiety about the time it takes them to orgasm or even come close to it thus, keeping them from getting there. The average woman requires about 20 minutes of foreplay, low intensity arousal before any form of an estimate of 20 minutes of continued clitoral stimulation in order to reach orgasm with their partner. If you are a heterosexual male reading this or a bisexual or lesbian female, remind yourself of the "20/20 Rule" when you seek to please your female partner. As a female reader, understand that you shouldn't judge yourself for taking the time you need to reach arousal. As a reminder to heterosexual men and women, we need to leave the obsession with a "vaginal orgasm" and understand that women primarily climax with clitoral stimulation (an estimate of 15% of women can reach climax via vaginal stimulation alone.) Foreplay is key for women, and the word itself is a bit of a misnomer for women as we don't really consider it a prelude to sex, it can oftentimes be the best part of sex! Most male partners are extremely open to more foreplay and genuinely want to do what makes their female partner feel pleasure and closeness. However, there are men out there that just don't understand the mechanics of female sexual pleasure and believe that the vagina is like an "inside out penis" which can receive pleasure with intercourse. One therapist quotes in their book, "Try to imagine sex 3x a week, 50 weeks a year, for 12 years - only thrusting never climaxing" (Great Sex, Castleman.) The pressure for women to orgasm can hurt both of you in multiple ways. Some men are disappointed that their partner doesn't orgasm because they feel it says something about their sexual skill or physical attractiveness. This can bring the woman further anxiety about not reaching climax because she feels she will upset him or he will feel unloved if she doesn't climax.

Male pressure for the female orgasm can be a misconception of sexual appetites and love. Perhaps he feels that she needs to "want it" as much as he does to pursue her or to feel reciprocal or ok with asking for sex. A lesson I have had to share with each and every one of my male partners so far is that even though I don't feel I can orgasm or even want to orgasm, I want to show love and affection in some way to him. I never do anything I don't want to do or am uncomfortable with but more often than not, I want to express my feelings sexually without the expectation of my orgasm. It can seem a foreign concept to them at first, particularly younger men, who perhaps not have been with many women or who have been with women who have a culture of faking it out of fear. Most women, when asked and able to answer candidly will tell you that quickies without orgasmic reciprocation, oral sex, or manual stimulation are ways that they prefer to show passion and affection to their lover without the pressure of their own orgasm. If you are one of those lucky women who have orgasms more often than not, I tip my hat to you, envy you, and applaud you. Keep on doing what you're doing, and read on for tips that are more applicable for your situation. If you are not, work with your partner to communicate these statistics, research and explain how you are one of many women who feel this way. Ensure he doesn't attach your orgasm with your desire for sex and intimacy or his own sexual worth. Work towards orgasm as a goal but slowly and with his understanding of the female arousal cycle and timing. A great book for both of you to read is The Female Brain as well as its counterpart, The Male Brain. These can give you a light prose version of the neurochemical biological differences between men and women in addition to our sexual response and feelings of attachment. It can take some of the emotional baggage out of the effort to understand one another when it is written out the way it is through science and research. Both books are very easy reads and are great topics for conversation.

CHAPTER 27

IN CLOSING

Of course not all of these tips are one size fits all. There are many that are dependent on the level of discomfort one or both of you is experiencing. Some may not be realistic or appropriate for your relationship situation or their limits. However, I believe that there are many here worth trying for most couples who want to get a boost to the passion and fire in their relationship. The fact that you are reading this text demonstrates your willingness to make and effort and seek resolution, happiness, and harmony. You are working to become an educated lover. Read voraciously, make the effort, share resources, and encourage you partner to do the same. Prioritize the expansion of your minds and hearts. You are working towards a better solution and sexual rhythm with your partner. Don't give up on yourselves if one idea fails to help, please keep trying. Between lovers, sometimes the effort is all it takes to remind each other that there is excitement and tenderness under the difficulty.

References

Bradberry, Greaves (2009). *Emotional Intelligence 2.0*. San Diego: TalentSmart.

Eric R. Bressler, & Rod R. Martin (2006). Production and appreciation of humor as sexually selected traits, Evolution & Human Behavior, Volume 27, Issue 2, Pages 121–130.

Call, V., Sprecher, S., & Schwartz, P. (1995).The incidence and frequency of marital sex in a national sample. Journal of marriage and family, 57(3), 639-652. http://www.jstor.org/stable/353919

Gary Chapman (1995). The Five Love Languages: How to Express Heartfelt Commitment to Your Mate. Northfield Publishing. ISBN 1881273156.

Leitenberg, H., & Hicks, T. V. (2001). Sexual fantasies about one's partner versus someone else: Gender differences in incidence and frequency. The Journal of Sex Research, 38, 43-50.

The Myers-Briggs Foundation

http://www.myersbriggs.org/type-use-for-everyday-life/psychological-type-and-relationships/

National Survey of Sexual Health and Behavior (NSSHB). Findings from the National Survey of Sexual Health and Behavior, Centre for Sexual Health Promotion, Indiana University.Journal of Sexual Medicine,Vol. 7, Supplement 5.

Emotional Intelligence Test

http://www.emotionalintelligence.net/

Nielsen

http://www.nielsen.com/us/en/insights/reports/2014/an-era-of-growth-the-cross-platform-report.html

Other Recommended Reading

Great Sex: A Man's Guide to the Secret Principles of Total-Body Sex, by Michael Castleman

Wanting Sex Again: How to Rediscover Your Desire and Heal a Sexless Marriage by Laurie Watson

The Female Brain, by Louann Brizendine

The Male Brain, by Louann Brizendine

https://www.psychologytoday.com/blog/married-and-still-doing-it, Blog by Laurie Watson

WAIT! – DO YOU LIKE FREE BOOKS?

My **FREE Gift** to You!! As a way to say **Thank You** for downloading my book, I'd like to offer you more **FREE BOOKS!** Each time we release a NEW book, we offer it first to a small number of people as a test - drive. Because of your commitment here in downloading my book, I'd love for you to be a part of this group. You can join easily here → **http://www.rochellefoxx.com**

ALSO CHECK OUT MY OTHER #1

BESTSELLING BOOK – "Sex and Marriage – Discover 10 Ways to Turn Your Sex Life from Routine to Lustful Desire" here

→ http://www.amazon.com/dp/B00V2MO0RY

BONUS FOR THE LADIES

A must watch - The Single Most Important Thing To A Man . . .

It takes a lot to shock me, but this video made me go "Wow."

===>> http://tinyurl.com/l8usq4y

It's by this guy named James Bauer and it explains the single most important thing to a man when it comes to having a relationship.

===>> http://tinyurl.com/l8usq4y

If you think guys are "complicated" or "hard to figure out" you really need to watch this video now.

Your Fire Lover,

Rochelle Foxx

P.S. After he reveals the "most important thing," James shows you how to trigger this one critical emotion in your guy to draw him closer to you and make him almost addicted to you long term.

What I really love about what James says is that it's not manipulative or "game playing."

===>> http://tinyurl.com/l8usq4y

BONUS FOR THE GUYS

(Ladies you will LOVE this too)

Below is my #1 Recommended Program for my ALL Male Clients.

I have never recommended any other program over this one.

Listen to me guys…

3 Things You Can Do To A Woman To Give Her The Best Orgasms Of Her Life

Do your wife a favor and go to this link.

http://tinyurl.com/k6k6xjf

Conclusion

Thank you again for downloading this book!

If you enjoyed this book, then I'd like to ask you for a favor, would you be kind enough to leave a review for this book on Amazon? It'd be greatly appreciated!

Help us better serve you by sending questions or comments to rochellefoxxbooks@gmail.com - Thank you!

Made in the USA
Middletown, DE
23 August 2015